KARL ROVE:

Inside the Mind of a Political Genius

Gerard A. Jones

Karl Rove

Karl Rove

TABLE OF CONTENTS

Karl Rove

INTRODUCTION

Karl Rove is one of the most influential people in the complex and dynamic world of American politics. Being a strong tactician, a master strategist, and a divisive figure in his own right, Rove has left a legacy that goes beyond simple party affiliation. He is a fascinating figure who is hated by some for being a cunning manipulator and praised by others as a political genius. But whatever one's viewpoint, there is no denying the fascination that surrounds the man known as The Architect of contemporary political campaigns.

The goal of this book, Karl Rove: Inside the Mind of a Political Genius, is to take readers on a profound journey inside the mind of this fascinating individual. It does this by dissecting the intricacies of his political maneuvers, studying the methods that underlie them, and investigating the long-term effects of his decisions on the political climate in America. We set out on a quest to comprehend the inner workings of one of the most significant political brains of our time through painstaking research, open interviews, and perceptive analysis.

Rove's ascent to fame was quite extraordinary. From his early years as a young political operative in Texas to his crucial position as George W. Bush's top strategist throughout his two presidential campaigns, Rove's career was characterized by ambition, shrewdness, and an unwavering will to change the political environment to suit his preferences. Along the way, he invented the use of data and analytics, transformed campaign strategies, and skillfully used his power to garner praise and scorn.

But beneath Rove's strategic genius is a complicated, sometimes contradictory person. Claims of brutality and dishonesty contrast with his image as a mastermind. His pursuit of authority and influence is occasionally tempered by periods of weakness and reflection. Furthermore, his lasting reputation is tarnished by scandals, disputes, and the ongoing discussion about how much he contributed to the direction of American politics.

Rove the strategist, Rove the ideologue, Rove the tactician, and Rove the provocateur will all come up as we read through the chapters in this book. We'll look at the key events that shaped his career, the conflicts he engaged in, the wins he achieved, and the losses he suffered. Throughout it all, we will try to understand what makes Karl Rove a phenomenon—a force to be reckoned with in the annals of American history—rather than just a political figure.

Come along with us as we take a look inside the thoughts and emotions of Karl Rove, a man whose legacy will continue to define American politics and whose influence can still be felt in the halls of power.

Karl Rove

"Karl Rove: Inside the Mind of a Political Genius" is a
welcome addition

CHAPTER 1:WHO IS KARL ROVE

American political strategist, pundit, and consultant Karl Rove is well-known. He became well-known for his contributions as President George W. Bush's principal counselor while Bush was in the White House. Bush's political campaigns and legislative agenda are frequently attributed to Rove, who gained the moniker "The Architect" for his astute political maneuvering.

Born in Denver, Colorado on December 25, 1950, Rove grew up in Texas and was active in Republican politics from an early age. After enrolling at the University of Utah, he subsequently moved to the University of Texas at Austin, where he completed his political science degree. Early in his political career, Rove held positions within the Republican Party and contributed to several Republican elections.

Karl Rove

In the 1990s, Rove gained notoriety as a political strategist and adviser. He was instrumental in George W. Bush's victories in his campaigns for governor of Texas in 1994 and 1998, as well as in 2000 and 2004. During the Bush administration, Rove held the positions of Senior Advisor and Deputy Chief of Staff, giving him significant influence over choices about both foreign and domestic policy.

Throughout his career, Rove has been renowned for his ability to rally conservative voters, his mastery of political communications, and his data-driven approach to campaigning. But he has also drawn criticism and controversy, especially for his actions during election campaigns and his involvement in several political scandals.

Following his departure from the White House, Rove continued to be involved in Republican politics as a consultant, pundit, and commentator. In addition to writing multiple books on politics and history, he has continued to share his ideas on political strategy with a variety of media venues.

Karl Rove's impact on American politics is well known, and his career has had a long-lasting effect on the country's political climate. He is still a divisive figure, reviled by some for his contentious methods and policies and adored by many for his political savvy.

1.1 Formative Years

On December 25, 1950, Karl Rove was born in Denver, Colorado, the son of Reba Wood and Louis Claude Rove Jr. A few times after his birth, his family relocated to Salt Lake City, Utah. Among the difficulties Rove had as a child was the divorce of his parents when he was only 19 years old. Being mostly raised by his mother, Rove grew up with a strong sense of self-reliance and fortitude.

Karl Rove

Rove thrived academically and showed an early interest in politics despite the challenges at home. While attending Olympus High School in Salt Lake City, he showed a talent for political organizing and got involved in student government. Rove's teenage years were marked by a growing enthusiasm for politics that shaped his future aspirations.

Rove studied political science at the University of Utah after enrolling there after high school. But he quickly changed schools, attending the University of Texas in Austin because of the state's conservative vibe and active political culture. Rove immersed himself in conservative ideas and served as chairman of the College Republicans at UT Austin, where he got heavily involved in student politics.

During his time in college, Rove's political involvement attracted the interest of powerful Republicans. He made a name for himself as a brilliant strategist and organizer right away, becoming well-known for his unwavering work ethic and keen intelligence. Rove's early involvement in grassroots politics served as a springboard for his work as a political adviser and operator.

During his early years, Rove was driven by a strong desire to succeed in politics and a strong commitment to conservative ideals. His early experiences gave him a strong sense of resolve and perseverance that would be useful to him in the future. Rove took the lessons from his childhood and the ideals taught by his family and mentors with him when he set out on his career as a professional politician.

1.2 Education

Karl Rove studied with an intensity commensurate with his growing political interest. Following his graduation from Salt Lake City, Utah's Olympus High School, Rove enrolled at the University of Utah to start his undergraduate career. He eventually changed schools, finishing his undergraduate studies in political science at the University of Texas at Austin, where he felt the atmosphere was more supportive of his conservative political views.

Rove was a rising star in college politics at the University of Texas. He became actively involved in the College Republicans group and became chairman at some point. His service as a College Republican leader prepared him for his eventual career in politics by giving him invaluable expertise in political strategy and organization.

Rove's learning went beyond the classroom as he engaged in real-world political activities. Through active participation in local and state political campaigns, he developed his talents in grassroots organization, campaign management, and fundraising. His grasp of the inner workings of American politics was shaped by this practical experience, which complemented his academic studies.

Karl Rove

Rove pursued his scholarly goals in addition to his political efforts, even after his early success and involvement in politics. He had a sharp mind and a voracious desire for knowledge while he was a student at the University of Texas, traits that would come in handy for him later in life.

Rove's education extended beyond his time as a student. A lifelong student of professional development and self-improvement, he kept adding to his knowledge and experience. His never-ending curiosity and unwavering commitment to becoming an expert in his field drove him to look for growth and learning opportunities at every point in his career.

In the end, Karl Rove's education was a complex process that included both formal academic coursework and real-world political experience. While his active participation in college politics and practical experience in political campaigns offered priceless lessons in strategy, leadership, and the nuances of the American political system, his time at the University of Texas gave him a strong foundation in political science. All of these encounters helped to mold Rove into the capable political adviser and strategist he would eventually become.

CHAPTER 2: Political Career

Karl Rove's significant position as a Republican Party strategist and counselor, especially during George W. Bush's administration, has been a defining feature of his political career. An outline of his political career is provided below:

1. Early Political Engagement: While still a student, Rove started his political career in the late 1960s and early 1970s. He worked on Texas political campaigns and held several positions within the College Republicans before becoming heavily involved in conservative issues and Republican politics.

2. Strategic Consulting: In the 1970s and 1980s, Rove made a name for himself as a proficient political consultant by contributing to several local, state, and federal Republican campaigns. He became known for his

data-driven strategy, strategic thinking, and capacity to galvanize conservative voters.

3. Work with George W. Bush: After meeting the president in the early 1970s, Rove's most significant political alliance was with him. Bush's triumphant campaigns for Texas governor in 1994 and 1998, as well as his presidential bids in 2000 and 2004, were greatly aided by Rove. Bush's election triumphs were greatly aided by Rove's organizational prowess and strategic direction.

4. Senior Advisor to President Bush: Rove joined the White House as Deputy Chief of Staff and Senior Advisor following Bush's 2000 election. He had a great deal of influence over decisions about foreign and domestic policy in this capacity. Rove was well-known for having influenced Bush's political agenda, which included national security, education, and tax policies.

5. Use of Analytics and Data: Rove was a pioneer in promoting the use of analytics and data in political

campaigns. Using voter and demographic data, he developed novel methods for organizing voters and identifying important battlegrounds. He also customized messages for target audiences.

6. Disputations and Reactions: Rove's political career was not devoid of disagreements. His involvement in several political scandals, like as the Valerie Plame affair, which entailed the disclosure of sensitive information, brought him criticism. Rove was also charged with using slanderous techniques and dividing the political opposition.

7. Career After Leave: After leaving the White House in 2007, Rove continued to be involved in Republican politics as a consultant, pundit, and commentator. He developed into a well-known figure in the conservative movement and persisted in sharing his political strategy insights with a variety of media platforms.

In general, Karl Rove's political career is distinguished by his ability to strategize, his clout inside the

Republican Party, and his part in reshaping American politics under the George W. Bush presidency. Rove continues to be a prominent figure in American politics despite disagreements and criticism.

2.1 Initial Involvement in Politics

Karl Rove's early political career began in his early years, during which he showed a strong interest in Republican politics and conservative causes. A closer look at his early political endeavors is provided below:

1. College Republican Leadership: Rove got very involved in the College Republicans group while he was a student at the University of Texas at Austin. He moved up the ranks fast and soon held the title of College Republicans chairman, which gave him the ability to plan political rallies, encourage student turnout, and promote conservative values on campus.

2. Campaign labor: Rove got his start in real-world political labor by volunteering on several Republican campaigns even before he had his college degree. His political operator abilities were sharpened as a result of the practical experience he obtained in voter engagement, grassroots organizing, and campaign administration.

3. Engagement in Texas Politics: The majority of Rodve's early political endeavors took place in Texas, where he made contacts with members of the Republican Party of the state. He gained experience as a committed and successful political strategist by working on several municipal and state-level campaigns.

4. Strategic Consulting: Key Republicans were quickly drawn to Rove because of his organizational skills and strategic intuition. He started working as a political consultant, giving campaigns and candidates advice on voter targeting, messaging, and strategy.

5. Alignment with Conservative Ideology: Rove never wavered in his dedication to conservative ideals and principles during his early political career. The conservative movement of the 1960s and 1970s had a significant impact on him, as he adopted ideas of limited government, free-market economics, and conventional social values.

6. Networking and Mentoring: Rove's early political career was distinguished by his skill at networking and his capacity to establish connections with influential Republicans. To help him navigate the complicated world of politics, he looked for mentors.

All things considered, Karl Rove's early political involvement prepared the way for his successful future as a political advisor and strategist. His involvement in campaign work, college politics, and strategic consulting gave him important insights and abilities that would influence his future political philosophy.

2.2 Working with George W. Bush

Karl Rove and George W. Bush forged one of the most important alliances in the annals of contemporary American politics. From his successful campaigns for Texas governor to his presidency, Bush's political career was significantly shaped by Rove's strategic acumen. The following summarizes Rove's involvement with George W. Bush:

1. Early Alliance: While both were active in Texas politics in the early 1970s, Rove and George W. Bush first came into contact with one another. They had similar views on the future of the Republican Party and conservatism. When they worked together on numerous political projects over the years, their alliance would only get stronger.

2. Gubernatorial Campaigns: In both the 1994 and 1998 campaigns of George W. Bush for governor of Texas, Rove was a key figure. In his capacity as Bush's

principal advisor and strategist, Rove developed a winning plan that highlighted the president's track record as a prosperous businessman as well as his ideas for conservative governance and educational reform.

3. Innovative Campaigning: Rove's style of campaigning was distinguished by strategic thinking and inventiveness. He was a trailblazer in the application of data and analytics to political campaigns, using voter demographic data to target important constituencies and customize messages for particular audiences. Rove's skill with campaign strategies contributed to Bush's wins in both of the gubernatorial contests.

4. Presidential Campaigns: George W. Bush's triumphant presidential campaigns in 2000 and 2004 represented Rove's pinnacle accomplishment. In his capacity as Bush's principal political strategist, Karl Rove oversaw carefully thought-out campaigns that made the most of Bush's advantages as a charismatic speaker and leader. Bush's election victories were made possible in large part

by Rove's strategic vision and organizational prowess in navigating the complexities of national politics.

5. Policy Influence: In addition to his work as a campaign strategist, Karl Rove had a significant impact on Bush administration policy choices. He was instrumental in forming Bush's domestic agenda as Senior Advisor and Deputy Chief of Staff, particularly the policies about healthcare, education reform, and taxes. Many of the administration's initiatives bore Rove's fingerprints, demonstrating his extensive involvement in both political and policy matters.

6. Legacy and Impact: Rove and George W. Bush's alliance permanently altered the course of American politics. Collectively, they transformed the Republican Party and ushered in a period of conservative rule. Rove gained the moniker "The Architect" and cemented his status as one of the most significant political operatives of his era thanks to his astute political maneuvering and steadfast devotion to Bush.

Karl Rove

In conclusion, Karl Rove's collaboration with George W. Bush is a pivotal moment in American political history as well as a defining chapter in the careers of both men. Their cooperation was a prime example of the value of strategic planning, capable leadership, and a common future vision.

2.3 The Deputy Chief of Staff Position

Karl Rove's tenure as George W. Bush's deputy chief of staff was an extension of his long-standing alliance with the president, which was characterized by influence over politics and policy. An examination of Rove's time as Deputy Chief of Staff is provided below:

1. Strategic Advisor: Rove remained one of President Bush's most trusted advisors while serving as Deputy Chief of Staff, offering strategic advice on a variety of matters. Rove was an indispensable asset in negotiating

the intricate terrain of Washington politics because of his sharp political instincts and profound knowledge of the American electorate.

2. Policy Development: Although Rove's main reputation came from his political savvy, he was also instrumental in forming the Bush administration's policy platform. He collaborated closely with other high-ranking officials to create and carry out important programs, especially in the fields of economic policy, healthcare, and education reform.

3. Political Liaison: Rove played a pivotal role in facilitating communication between the White House and other political players, such as members of Congress, governors of individual states, and prominent figures in the Republican Party. He advanced the administration's legislative agenda and garnered support for its policy priorities by using his wide network of contacts and persuasive skills.

4. Election Strategy: Rove continued to be heavily involved in political strategy even in his capacity as Deputy Chief of Staff, especially in the run-up to the 2006 midterm elections. To keep the Republican Party in control of Congress, he was instrumental in formulating the party's campaign strategy. But the Republican Party suffered huge defeats in the 2006 elections, and Rove left the White House not long after.

5. Legacy and Controversies: There was some controversy surrounding Rove's time as deputy chief of staff. His involvement in several political scandals, like as the Valerie Plame affair, which entailed the disclosure of sensitive information, brought him criticism. Opponents and watchdog organizations also focused attention on Rove because of his aggressive political strategies and apparent partisanship.

6. Post-White House Career: Rove remained involved in Republican politics as a commentator, columnist, and consultant after leaving the White House in 2007. He continued to be a well-known figure in the conservative

movement and to share his political strategy insights with the media.

All things considered, Karl Rove's position as George W. Bush's Deputy Chief of Staff demonstrated his dual emphasis on politics and policy. His political astuteness and strategic direction had a profound effect on American politics in general and the Bush administration in particular.

CHAPTER 3: Political Strategy and Tactics

Karl Rove is well known for his sophisticated, impactful, and occasionally contentious political strategies and tactics. This is a synopsis of his methodology:

1. Data-Driven Campaigning: Rove was one of the first politicians to use analytics and data in their campaigns. Acknowledging the significance of voter demographic data, he employed advanced voter targeting strategies to pinpoint important constituencies and customize messages for particular audiences. By using a data-driven strategy, Rove was able to better mobilize voters and make the most of his campaign's resources.

2. Microtargeting: Based on behavioral, geographic, and demographic traits, Rove developed the first methods of microtargeting, which entails dividing the electorate into small, precisely defined groups. In crucial battlegrounds,

Karl Rove

Rove successfully engaged voters and increased turnout by focusing outreach efforts and messages on particular voter segments.

Rove highlighted the significance of message discipline in political communication in point three. To create concise, coherent messaging that connected with voters and reaffirmed important campaign themes, he worked closely with candidates and campaigns. By emphasizing message discipline, Rove was able to craft a cohesive narrative that resonated with voters from a variety of demographic backgrounds.

4. Negative Campaigning: When required, Rove did not hesitate to use negative campaigning strategies. He was aware of the influence that negative messaging and attack advertisements had on defining opponents and influencing public opinion. Although opponents frequently criticized Rove for his calculated use of negative advertising, it was successful in weakening opponents and changing the nature of close contests.

5 Long-Term Strategic Planning: Rome was renowned for his capacity for long-term strategic planning and his ability to predict political developments several steps ahead of time. He realized that careful planning and execution over several months or even years was necessary for campaigns to be successful. Because of his strategic vision, Rove was able to foresee obstacles, seize opportunities, and adjust to shifting political circumstances.

6. Coalition Building: Rove understood the value of forming alliances in the electoral process. He made an effort to assemble broad-based support coalitions from a range of political, interest, and demographic groups. Rove's success in winning elections and furthering conservative causes was largely attributed to his ability to form alliances and bring disparate factions together under a single political banner.

7. Utilization of Media and Technology: Rove was a pioneer in the field of utilizing new media and technology in elections. He was aware of the influence

direct mail, online communication, and television advertising had on voters and public opinion. By utilizing media and technology in novel ways, Rove modernized political campaigning and established new benchmarks for electoral communication.

All things considered, Karl Rove's political strategy and tactics are a blend of creativity, pragmatism, and unwavering resolve. There is no doubting the influence of Rove's strategic brilliance on American politics and the enduring legacy of his campaigns, even though some have criticized his methods.

3.1 Strategies for Campaigning

Karl Rove is renowned for his innovative campaigning techniques, which have revolutionized political strategy in the modern era. Here are some key elements of Rove's campaigning techniques:

Karl Rove

1. Data Analysis and Microtargeting: Rove was an early proponent of using data analysis to target specific voter demographics. He employed sophisticated voter databases and analytics to identify swing voters, understand their preferences, and tailor campaign messages to resonate with their interests. This microtargeting approach allowed Rove to maximize the impact of campaign resources and focus efforts where they were most likely to yield results.

2. Message Discipline: Rove emphasized the importance of maintaining a consistent message throughout the campaign. He worked closely with candidates to develop clear, compelling narratives that highlighted their strengths and contrasted them with their opponents. This message discipline helped to create a unified campaign narrative that resonated with voters and reinforced key themes.

3. Negative Advertising: While controversial, Rove was not afraid to use negative advertising as a strategic tool in his campaigns. He understood the power of negative

messaging to shape public opinion and define opponents. Rove's campaigns often employed attack ads that criticized opponents' records or character, seeking to weaken their support and undermine their credibility.

4. Ground Game and Voter Mobilization: Rove recognized the importance of building a strong ground game to turn out supporters on Election Day. He invested heavily in grassroots organizing, deploying volunteers to knock on doors, make phone calls, and engage with voters in key battlegrounds. Rove's focus on voter mobilization helped to drive turnout among supportive demographics and secure electoral victories.

5. Strategic Alliances and Coalition Building: Rove understood the value of building broad-based coalitions of support to win elections. He forged alliances with various interest groups, advocacy organizations, and political constituencies, seeking to unite disparate factions under a common political banner. Rove's coalition-building efforts helped to broaden the appeal of his candidates and expand their electoral reach.

6. Media Management: Rove was skilled at managing media relations and controlling the narrative of his campaigns. He worked closely with journalists to shape news coverage and frame the debate on key issues. Rove's ability to effectively communicate his candidates' messages through traditional and new media channels helped to shape public opinion and influence voter perceptions.

Overall, Karl Rove's campaigning techniques reflect a combination of strategic acumen, data-driven decision-making, and a willingness to employ aggressive tactics when necessary. While controversial, Rove's methods have had a profound impact on modern political strategy and continue to shape the way campaigns are run in the digital age.

3.2 Use of Data and Analytics

Karl Rove

Karl Rove's use of data and analytics in political campaigning revolutionized the way campaigns are conducted. Here's how he utilized these tools to gain a strategic advantage:

1. Voter Targeting: Rove understood that not all voters are equal in their potential impact on an election. He used data analysis to identify key demographic groups, including swing voters and undecided, and focused campaign efforts on persuading and mobilizing them. By targeting specific segments of the electorate, Rove could allocate resources more efficiently and maximize the impact of campaign messaging.

2. Voter Profiling: Rove employed sophisticated voter profiling techniques to understand the preferences, behaviors, and motivations of different voter groups. By analyzing demographic data, voting histories, consumer habits, and other factors, Rove developed detailed profiles of individual voters and used this information to craft personalized campaign messages tailored to their interests and concerns.

3. Predictive Modeling: Rove was an early adopter of predictive modeling techniques, which use historical data to forecast future outcomes. He used statistical analysis to predict voter behavior, assess the competitiveness of electoral districts, and identify strategic opportunities for his candidates. This predictive modeling allowed Rove to anticipate trends, allocate resources strategically, and make informed decisions about where to focus campaign efforts.

4. Direct Voter Contact: Rove prioritized direct voter contact as a key strategy for winning elections. He used data analysis to identify potential supporters and opponents, then deployed targeted outreach efforts, such as door-to-door canvassing, phone banking, and personalized mailers, to engage with voters on a one-on-one basis. This direct voter contact helped to build relationships, persuade undecided voters, and mobilize supporters to turn out on Election Day.

5. Message Testing: Rove conducted rigorous testing of campaign messages and advertisements to gauge their effectiveness with target audiences. He used focus groups, surveys, and polling data to assess which messages resonated most strongly with voters and adjusted campaign strategies accordingly. This iterative process of message testing allowed Rove to refine campaign messaging and optimize its impact on voter perceptions.

6. Real-Time Data Analysis: Rove emphasized the importance of real-time data analysis in monitoring and adjusting campaign strategies on the fly. He used polling data, voter turnout statistics, and other metrics to track the progress of his campaigns, identify emerging trends, and make tactical adjustments as needed. This agility in response to changing circumstances allowed Rove to stay ahead of the curve and adapt to evolving political dynamics.

Overall, Karl Rove's use of data and analytics transformed political campaigning into a more data-driven and scientifically rigorous endeavor. By harnessing the power of data analysis, Rove was able to gain a strategic advantage, target resources more effectively, and ultimately win elections for his candidates. His pioneering use of data and analytics continues to influence political strategy and campaign tactics to this day.

3.3 Policy Influence

While Karl Rove is primarily known for his prowess as a political strategist and campaign advisor, he also had significant influence over policy decisions during his time as Deputy Chief of Staff in the George W. Bush administration. Here's how Rove exerted policy influence:

1. Agenda Setting: Rove played a crucial role in setting the policy agenda for the Bush administration. He worked closely with President Bush to identify key

priorities and initiatives, shaping the administration's focus on issues such as tax cuts, education reform, healthcare, and national security. Rove's strategic guidance helped to define the administration's policy objectives and establish a clear direction for governance.

2. Policy Development: Rove was involved in the development and implementation of various policy initiatives across a wide range of issue areas. He worked with other senior officials and policy experts to craft legislative proposals, draft executive orders, and formulate regulatory policies. Rove's fingerprints could be seen on many of the administration's signature policy achievements, reflecting his influence over the policymaking process.

3. Political Considerations: Rove was keenly aware of the political implications of policy decisions and sought to align policy priorities with the administration's broader political goals. He understood the importance of policy successes in bolstering the administration's political standing and advancing its electoral interests.

Karl Rove

Rove's strategic approach to policymaking often took into account the potential electoral impact of policy initiatives and the need to appeal to key constituencies.

4. Messaging and Communication: Rove played a central role in communicating the administration's policy agenda to the public and shaping the narrative surrounding key policy initiatives. He worked closely with the White House communications team to develop messaging strategies, coordinate media outreach efforts, and frame policy debates in a way that resonated with voters. Rove's ability to effectively communicate the administration's policies helped to build public support and shape public opinion.

5. Coalition Building: Rove understood the importance of building broad-based coalitions of support to advance the administration's policy agenda. He worked to forge alliances with lawmakers, interest groups, advocacy organizations, and other stakeholders to build consensus around key policy priorities. Rove's coalition-building

efforts helped to overcome partisan divisions and secure legislative victories on behalf of the administration.

Overall, Karl Rove's policy influence was an integral part of his broader role as Deputy Chief of Staff in the Bush administration. While he may be best known for his political acumen and campaign expertise, Rove also played a significant role in shaping the administration's policy agenda and advancing its policy objectives. His political astuteness and strategic direction had a profound effect on American politics in general and the Bush administration in particular.

CHAPTER 4: Controversies and Criticism

Karl Rove's political career has been marked by controversy and criticism, stemming from his role as a prominent strategist and advisor within the Republican Party. Here are some of the key controversies and criticisms surrounding Rove:

1. Valerie Plame Affair: One of the most notable controversies involving Rove was his role in the Valerie Plame affair. In 2003, Plame, a CIA operative, was publicly identified in a newspaper column, leading to accusations that the Bush administration had leaked her identity as retribution for her husband's criticism of the Iraq War. Rove was investigated by a special prosecutor but was ultimately not charged with any wrongdoing, although the episode tarnished his reputation and raised questions about his ethics.

2. Use of Negative Campaigning: Rove has been criticized for his use of negative campaigning tactics, including attack ads and smear campaigns against political opponents. Critics argue that Rove's aggressive tactics contribute to polarization and negativity in political discourse, undermining trust in the electoral process and fostering cynicism among voters.

3. Accusations of Partisanship: Rove has been accused of using his influence for partisan purposes, prioritizing the electoral interests of the Republican Party over the public good. Critics argue that Rove's strategic calculations often prioritize winning elections at any cost, even if it means sacrificing principles or engaging in unethical behavior.

4. Involvement in Political Scandals: Rove's proximity to various political scandals during his time in the Bush administration has raised questions about his judgment and integrity. In addition to the Valerie Plame affair, Rove has been linked to controversies surrounding the firing of U.S. attorneys, the manipulation of intelligence

leading up to the Iraq War, and allegations of voter suppression and election fraud.

5. Accusations of Divisiveness: Rove's aggressive style of politics has been criticized for exacerbating divisions within American society. Critics argue that Rove's focus on winning elections through polarization and wedge issues has contributed to the erosion of civility and bipartisanship in politics, making it increasingly difficult to find common ground and address pressing issues facing the nation.

6. Lack of Accountability: Despite his involvement in numerous controversies, Rove has largely avoided facing consequences for his actions. Critics argue that Rove's ability to evade accountability underscores a broader problem of impunity and lack of accountability for powerful political operatives, allowing them to operate with impunity and undermine democratic norms.

Overall, Karl Rove's controversies and criticisms reflect the contentious nature of American politics and the polarizing impact of his strategic tactics. While he remains a polarizing figure, Rove's influence on American politics cannot be denied, and his legacy continues to shape political discourse and debate.

4.1 Involvement in Scandals

Karl Rove's involvement in various scandals during his time as a political strategist and advisor has been a subject of controversy and scrutiny. The following are a few significant scandals in which Rove has been involved:

1. The Valerie Plame controversy: The Valerie Plame affair was one of Karl Rove's most well-known controversies. Columnist Robert Novak made CIA operative Valerie Plame's covert status public in 2003. Members of the Bush administration were accused of masterminding the leak as payback for Ambassador Joseph Wilson, Plame's spouse, having openly criticized

the administration's rationale for the Iraq War. Rove's involvement in the leak was closely examined, even though he was never officially accused of anything.

2. U.S. Attorneys' Dismissal: In 2006, the Bush administration fired several U.S. attorneys; this dispute involved Rove. Critics claimed Rove and other administration officials fired the lawyers for political reasons, hoping to sway pending investigations and prosecutions for their political advantage. Despite Rove's denial of any role in the dismissals, his correspondence with the Justice Department about them prompted concerns about the administration's intentions.

3. Voter Suppression Allegations: Throughout several election cycles, Ron Paul has been implicated in attempts to stifle Democratic-leaning groups' ability to cast ballots. Critics claim that to prevent particular voter groups from casting ballots, Rove and other Republican organizers used strategies like voter intimidation, voter caging, and the dissemination of false information. Despite Rove's denial of any misconduct, these

accusations have raised questions about the fairness of the voting process.

4. Intelligence Manipulation: Rove was associated with the Bush administration's attempts to sway intelligence before the Iraq War. Critics claim that Rove and other administration officials misled the public about the justification for military involvement and inflated the threat posed by Iraq's WMDs. Even though Rove denied any misconduct, there is still discussion and examination surrounding the controversy regarding the administration's use of intelligence in the lead-up to the war.

5. Political Payback Allegations: Rove has been accused of taking political revenge on Bush administration opponents and detractors. Critics contend that Rove orchestrated smear operations against political rivals and used his influence to attack people and groups viewed as administration enemies. Rove also allegedly utilized government resources for partisan ends. Despite Rove's denial of these accusations, they have raised questions

about power abuse and unethical behavior in the political elite.

All things considered, Karl Rove's role in several controversies has called into question his morality, discernment, and honesty as a political operative. Despite his repeated denials of any wrongdoing, he has become a divisive figure in American politics due to his association with controversy and his reputation as a cunning political operative.

4.2 Manipulation Allegations

Karl Rove has faced accusations of manipulation during his tenure as a political strategist and advisor, especially concerning his influence on public opinion and election results. The following are some of the most prominent charges of Rove's manipulation:

Karl Rove

1. Manipulation of the Media: To further his political objectives and sway public opinion, Rode has been charged with manipulating the media. Critics contend that Rove has manipulated the information landscape, spread misinformation, and twisted stories to support his political candidates and agendas. This has sparked questions about the legitimacy of democracy and the media's ability to hold the powerful to account.

2. Voter Suppression: Rove has been accused of being involved in campaigns to discourage certain demographic groups from casting ballots, especially those who are inclined to support Democratic candidates. Critics contend that to deny voters their right to vote and sway elections in favor of their favorite candidates, Rove and other Republican operatives have used strategies like voter intimidation, voter caging, and the spread of false information. The fairness and integrity of the election process have come under scrutiny as a result of these charges.

3. Gerrymandering: Redrawing political districts to give one party the advantage over another is a tactic known as gerrymandering, and it has been connected to attempts by Romeve to alter electoral borders. Opponents contend that Rove has manipulated congressional districts to strengthen Republican advantage and weaken the voting power of minority groups. Concerns over the deterioration of democratic standards and the skewed representation in politics have been raised by this.

4. Negative Campaigning: Rove has come under fire for his employment of defamation lawsuits and attack commercials against political rivals. Opponents contend that Rove's aggressive strategies exacerbate political discourse's divisiveness and negativity, eroding voter confidence in the democratic process and encouraging cynicism. Concerns over the effects of negative campaigning on the state of democracy and the caliber of public discourse have been raised by this.

5. Policy Debate Distortion: Rove has come under fire for allegedly manipulating policy discussions to further

ideological agendas and party goals. Critics claim that Rove has framed policy issues through his influence in a way that is advantageous to his candidates and marginalizes those who hold different opinions. Concerns have been expressed concerning special interests' influence on public policy and the capacity of elected leaders to rule in the public interest.

Karl Rove's career has generally been marred by accusations of manipulation, which reflects larger worries about the role that partisanship, money, and power play in American politics. Even though Rove has continuously denied any wrongdoing, these allegations have fueled discussions about the need for increased accountability and transparency in government as well as the integrity of the democratic process.

4.3 Reactions and Retaliations

Karl Rove

Karl Rove has addressed the problems surrounding his political career with several defenses and explanations in response to charges and criticisms made against him. Here are a few typical reactions and counterarguments:

1. Denial of Wrongdoing: Regarding the scandals and controversies he has been involved in, Rode has continuously refuted any wrongdoing or improper behavior. He has insisted that he followed the law and moral principles and has dismissed accusations of wrongdoing as the product of opponents' political vendettas.

2. Attribution of Partisan Motives: Rove has frequently claimed that his opponents' criticism of him is motivated by partisanship, claiming that their goal is to damage his reputation and diminish his political power for their political advantage. He has presented himself as the victim of political persecution and portrayed the charges against him as part of a larger party conflict.

3. Emphasis on Legal Compliance: In his political activities and campaign operations, Rove has made it clear that he has complied with all applicable laws and regulations. In an attempt to soften the blow of criticism, he has said that he has followed the letter of the law and has not participated in any unlawful activity.

4. Concentrate on Results: As proof of his efficacy as a political strategist and advisor, Rove has cited his history of winning elections and achieving legislative goals. He has emphasized the successes he has assisted in securing for his candidates and causes, highlighting the beneficial effects of his strategic advice on the results of elections and the formulation of public policy.

5. Appeal to Free Speech: Rove has defended his employment of aggressive political strategies and negative campaigning techniques as legitimate forms of political expression and free speech. He has maintained that his strategies are lawful political communication covered by the First Amendment and that intense

political competition and debate are necessary components of democracy.

6. Acknowledgment of Mistakes: Although Rove has consistently maintained his denials of misconduct, he has on occasion admitted to making mistakes or poor decisions in certain circumstances. But rather than portraying these errors as symptomatic of larger problems, he has usually played down the importance of these errors.

Throughout his political career, Karl Rove has generally used a range of rebuttals and defenses to handle criticisms and issues. Even while he has resisted accusations, he has also made an effort to shift the focus, lessen the impact of bad press, and hold onto his position as a significant figure in the Republican Party and conservative movement.

CHAPTER 5: Post-Government Career

Karl Rove entered a post-government career after leaving the White House in 2007 and has since held several positions in activism, media, and consultancy. Highlights from Rove's post-government career include the following:

1. Media Commentator: Rove rose to prominence as a political pundit, providing insights and viewpoints on elections, current affairs, and policy discussions. He was a commentator and political analyst on Fox News, among other television news programs, where he frequently made appearances. Media outlets looking for knowledgeable comments on political issues sought out Rove's observations and expertise.

2. Columnist: Rove is also well-known for his work as a columnist, penning essays and opinions for internet,

print, and magazine journals. He has written columns for magazines like The Wall Street Journal, giving his thoughts on a variety of political topics and events.

3. Author: Using his background as a political strategist and counselor, Rove has written multiple books on politics and public policy. His writings include political analysis (The Triumph of William McKinley: Why the Election of 1896 Still Matters) and memoirs (Courage and Consequence: My Life as a Conservative in the Fight).

4. Political Consulting: As a consultant and counselor, Rove has remained involved in Republican politics, offering candidates, campaigns, and political organizations strategic direction. Offering his skills in voter targeting, messaging, and campaign strategy, he has worked with candidates at the municipal, state, and federal levels.

5. Advocacy and Fundraising: To support conservative causes and candidates, Rove has taken part in several

advocacy and fundraising campaigns. He has ties to groups that have generated large quantities of money to back Republican politicians and causes, like American Crossroads and Crossroads GPS.

6. Political action: Rove continues to be a prominent member of the conservative movement and the Republican Party. He takes part in grassroots organization and political action. He has delivered speeches at conferences, political gatherings, and other events to encourage people to support conservative ideas and get involved in politics.

Karl Rove's post-government career has often been distinguished by his ongoing involvement in public affairs and politics. Rove continues to be a significant force in American politics and a well-known voice in the conservative movement as a media pundit, columnist, author, consultant, and supporter.

Karl Rove

5.1 Guidance and Counseling

Karl Rove has a long history of working as a political counselor and consultant, giving candidates, campaigns, and political organizations strategic direction. An outline of his advisory and consulting work is shown below:

1. Campaign Strategy: Rode is renowned for his proficiency in creating effective campaign plans. He collaborates closely with candidates to create all-inclusive campaign strategies that highlight their advantages, pinpoint crucial messaging, and target particular voter segments. With Rove's strategic advice, politicians can better negotiate the intricacies of contemporary political campaigns and increase their chances of winning elections.

2. Message Development: Rove helps politicians craft memorable, persuasive campaign statements that appeal to voters. He assists candidates in clearly communicating their beliefs, stances on issues, and future goals in a way that appeals to voters and sets them apart from their

rivals. Rove's skill in communications enables politicians to persuade unsure voters to support their candidacies.

3. Voter Targeting: To pinpoint important demographic groups and modify campaign outreach initiatives to appeal to them, Rove uses advanced voter targeting strategies. To identify swing votes, undecided, and other important populations, he conducts polls and analyses voter data. This enables campaigns to carefully spend resources and optimize their influence.

4. Media Strategy: Rove assists candidates in navigating the intricate world of traditional and digital media by offering advice on their media strategy. He helps candidates handle public relations, get positive media attention, and respond to questions and criticism from the media. Rove's experience in the media helps politicians sway public opinion and deliver their message.

5. Coalition Building: By interacting with a variety of interest groups and constituencies, Rove assists

candidates in forming wide coalitions of support. He helps candidates form partnerships with important constituencies, such as advocacy groups, elected officials, party leaders, and grassroots activists. Rove's efforts to forge coalitions aid politicians in growing their voter base and rallying support.

6. Strategic Counsel: Rove offers candidates counsel on a variety of political matters, such as opposition research, fundraising, crisis management, and debate preparation. He offers candidates helpful advice and insights into overcoming the difficulties of running for office by drawing on his vast political experience.

All in all, campaigns and candidates looking to obtain a political advantage have sought Karl Rove's consulting and advising services. His profound knowledge of American politics and his strategic acumen make him an invaluable resource for clients trying to win elections.

Karl Rove

5.2 Media Analysis

Karl Rove is a well-known television pundit who provides analysis and thoughts on elections, political developments, and policy discussions. An outline of Rove's media remarks is shown below:

1. Television Appearances: Rove has frequently appeared as a guest on news programs on television, offering analysis and opinion on a broad spectrum of political issues. He has given his opinion on current affairs, election outcomes, and policy discussions on networks like Fox News, CNN, MSNBC, and others. Viewers can get professional analysis and interpretation of breaking news and political developments via Rove's televised appearances.

2. Political Analysis: With years of expertise as a political strategist and counselor, Rove is renowned for his in-depth political analysis. He provides viewers with an understanding of election dynamics and the forces influencing political results by providing insights into

electoral trends, polling data, and campaign strategy. Rove is respected for his insightful, accurate, and in-depth political analysis.

In addition to his political analysis, Rove offers his viewpoint on legislative proposals, regulatory modifications, and other policy developments in his comments on policy matters. He contributes to discussions on immigration, national security, healthcare, taxation, and other important policy issues, giving viewers a well-informed analysis of the effects of policy choices on the nation.

4. Election Coverage: Rove is frequently asked to offer analysis on election outcomes, voter demographics, and the performance of political parties and candidates during election coverage. He helps viewers comprehend the significance of election results and their ramifications for the political climate and the future of the nation by giving them background information and understanding.

Karl Rove

5. Partisan Perspective: Rove frequently provides a partisan viewpoint in his media criticism because of his prominence in the Republican Party and conservative movement. He defends Republican candidates and officials pushes for conservative values and ideas, and criticizes Democratic attitudes and projects. With his partisan position, Rove gives viewers a variety of perspectives on political problems, adding complexity and diversity to the media landscape.

In general, audiences looking for a knowledgeable analysis and interpretation of political events and developments can benefit much from Karl Rove's media commentary. His knowledge, perceptiveness, and political viewpoint add to the diversity and depth of political discourse in the media.

CHAPTER 6:History and Significance

The influence and legacy of Karl Rove on US politics are profound and varied. An outline of his legacy and enduring influence is provided below:

1. Pioneering Political Strategy: With his revolutionary approach to campaigning and election victory, Karl Rove is widely recognized as a pioneer in the field of political strategy. His creative application of voter outreach, microtargeting, and data analytics changed the electoral environment and established new benchmarks for strategic campaigns.

2. Electoral Triumphs: At the municipal, state, and federal levels, Rove's tactical advice was crucial to the Republican candidates' multiple victories. His prowess in coalition building, voter mobilization, and message discipline helped Republicans win important

battlegrounds and keep control of Congress and the White House.

3. Partisan Polarization: Rove's combative strategies and unwavering commitment to securing victories in elections have exacerbated the already extreme polarization in American politics. He has increased partisanship, party stalemate, and intellectual polarization by using negative campaigns, attack commercials, and partisan messaging to foment division and hostility between Republicans and Democrats.

4. Policy Influence: In addition to his impact on politics, Rove has also had a major impact on policy making, helping to shape conservative agendas and objectives. His support of deregulation, tax reduction, and other conservative principles has influenced legislative discussions and shaped the course of government policy.

5. Media Presence: Rove has been able to mold public opinion and impact political discourse due to his media presence as a political analyst, columnist, and author,

which has increased his power and reach. His commentary adds to the variety of opinions in the media environment by offering a conservative take on current affairs and policy matters.

6. Controversies and Criticisms: Rove's legacy is not without controversy, as he has been called out for his aggressive campaign tactics and involvement in several political scandals. His reputation has been damaged and doubts regarding the integrity of American democracy have been aroused by accusations of partisanship, manipulation, and unethical behavior.

7. Republican Party Influence: Rove continues to be a significant force in the conservative movement and Republican Party, where his political acumen and strategic knowledge influence party policy and message. Republican contenders hoping to win and further conservative ideals are vying for his support and endorsement.

Karl Rove

Karl Rove left behind a complicated and wide-ranging legacy that has affected American politics in many ways. He is applauded for his electoral prowess and strategic acumen, but he is also chastised for encouraging partisan division and undermining democratic values. He still has an impact on discussions and choices made at the highest echelons of American politics.

6.1 Impact on Politics in America

Karl Rove has had a significant impact on American politics, influencing the approaches, methods, and procedures used in elections and the formulation of public policy. The following are some significant ways that Rove has impacted US politics:

1. Creative Campaigning Strategies: Rove is well known for his creative political campaigning strategies. His innovative use of voter outreach, microtargeting, and data analytics transformed the way elections are won and

campaigns are run. His focus on strategic planning and data-driven decision-making has raised the bar for campaign efficiency and effectiveness.

2. Partisan Strategy and Messaging: The Republican Party's messaging and objectives have been shaped in part by Rove's strategic advice. His focus on partisan division, message discipline, and negative campaigning has changed how Republicans engage their base and interact with voters. The growing polarization of American politics can be attributed to Rove's emphasis on winning elections at all costs.

3. Electoral Successes: Rove's political savvy has been instrumental in several Republican candidates' local, state, and national electoral successes. Republicans have won close races and kept control of Congress and the White House thanks to his skill in identifying swing voters, forming alliances, and increasing voter turnout.

4. Policy Influence: Rove's impact goes beyond politics into the realm of policymaking, where he has aided in

the advancement of Republican agendas and the shaping of the conservative policy agenda. His support of deregulation, tax reduction, and other conservative measures has impacted legislative discussions and determined the course of public policy.

5. Media Presence: Rode has increased his reach and influence through his work as a political analyst, author, and columnist. This has given him the ability to sway public opinion and direct political conversation. His commentary adds to the variety of opinions in the media environment by offering a conservative take on current affairs and policy matters.

6. Legacy of Controversy: Rove has been under fire for his use of aggressive campaign techniques and his role in several political scandals. His legacy is not without controversy. Although his reputation has been damaged by accusations of partisanship, manipulation, and unethical behavior, his influence in American politics has not decreased.

Karl Rove

All things considered, Karl Rove has had a profound and long-lasting impact on American politics. His media presence, partisanship, and strategic brilliance have had a long-lasting impact on American politics, influencing how elections are won, campaigns are managed, and laws are passed.

6.2 Assessment of Results

Karl Rove's accomplishments in the areas of political strategy, campaigning, and policy influence must be evaluated in light of both his accomplishments and failings. This is a fair assessment:

Successes:

1. Cutting-Edge Campaigning Strategies: Rove transformed political campaigning with his innovative use of voter engagement, microtargeting, and data analytics. His focus on data-driven decision-making and

strategic planning raised the bar for campaign efficacy and efficiency, helping Republican candidates win many electoral victories.

2. Electoral Successes: At the local, state, and federal levels, Rove was instrumental in helping Republican candidates win elections. His leadership in winning close contests and preserving Republican control of the House and Congress cemented his standing as a brilliant political strategist.

3. Political Strategy and Messaging: The Republican Party's messaging and agenda have been impacted by Rove's emphasis on message discipline, negative campaigning, and political divisiveness. The party's ideological unity and electoral success can be attributed to his strategic concentration on swing voters and energizing the party base.

4. Policy Influence: Rove's support of conservative policies, including deregulation, tax cuts, and national security initiatives, has altered legislative discussions

Karl Rove

and the course of governmental policy. During and
during his tenure in office, his strategic advice shaped
the conservative policy agenda and advanced Republican
agendas.

Drawbacks:

1. Controversies and Criticisms: Rove's legacy is
tarnished by controversy and criticism, especially in light
of his employment of aggressive campaign techniques
and his involvement in several political scandals. His
reputation has been damaged and doubts regarding the
integrity of American democracy have been aroused by
accusations of partisanship, manipulation, and unethical
behavior.

2. political Polarization: The growing polarization of
American politics can be attributed to Rove's
concentration on political messages and tactics. His
hostile campaigning and polarizing strategies have
exacerbated resentment between Republicans and

Democrats, increasing gridlock and eroding faith in public institutions.

3. Legacy of Division: Deepening divisiveness and divisions within American society are other hallmarks of the legacy left by Rove. His obsession with winning elections at all costs has made partisan victory more important than cooperation and compromise, which has fueled political polarization and radicalism.

4. Dubious Policy Choices: Despite Rove's considerable influence over policy discussions, some contend that his support of conservative policies has had detrimental effects on the nation. He has been controversial in his advocacy of tax reduction, deregulation, and military interventionism, which has produced contentious policy results.

In conclusion, Karl Rove has accomplished a great deal, especially in the areas of political strategy and winning elections. But controversy, criticism, and the continuation of party polarization in American politics also characterize his legacy. In assessing Rove's accomplishments, it is necessary to take into account both his advantages and disadvantages in influencing US politics.

CHAPTER 7: Personal Life

Even though Karl Rove is most recognized for his significant impact on American politics, there are facets of his personal life that provide light on the person who lies behind the political strategist. An outline of Karl Rove's private life is provided below:

1. Early Life and Education: On December 25, 1950, Karl Rove was born in Denver, Colorado. After his parents' divorce, he was reared by his mother and went to high school in Salt Lake City, Utah. Later, Rove enrolled in the University of Utah, but he chose to focus on his political career rather than earning a degree.

2. Family: Rove has had several marriages. In 1976, he got married for the first time to Valerie Wainwright, but they divorced. In 1986, he later wed Darby Tara Hickson, with whom he has a son. Rove divorced from his second marriage as well. Karen Johnson, a lobbyist

and former Texas deputy secretary of state, wed Rove in 2012.

3. Personal Interests: Rove has a wide range of interests outside of politics. He is well-known for being a voracious reader with a broad interest in literature, politics, and history. In addition, Rove enjoys listening to music, especially country and classical styles, and he can play the guitar.

Rove has experienced health difficulties all of his life, such as recurrent episodes of illness and issues with obesity. His detached retina required emergency surgery in 2010, which momentarily impaired his vision. Rove has continued to be involved in politics and public affairs despite these obstacles.

5. Philanthropy: Throughout his life, Rove has taken part in several charitable endeavors. Among other things, he has backed initiatives about veterans' affairs, healthcare, and education. Beyond the political sphere, Rove is

dedicated to improving society, as seen by his charitable activities.

6. Hobbies and Leisure: Hiking and cycling are two of Rove's favorite outdoor pursuits. He is also well-known for being a dog lover, and he has frequently been pictured with his furry friends.

All things considered, even though Karl Rove is most recognized for his influence and political career, his personal life provides insights into the complicated person behind the political strategist—a person with a wide range of interests, struggles in his personal life, and a dedication to changing politics and society at large.

7.1 Background and Family

Karl Rove's upbringing and influences are contextualized by his familial background. This is a synopsis:

Karl Rove

1. Influence from Family: Reba, Rove's mother, had a big impact on his childhood. She was a Democratic Party member who gave Rove an early interest in politics and current affairs. Rove remained close to his mother throughout his life, despite their political differences.

2. Education: Rove got interested in student politics while attending Salt Lake City, Utah, high school. Later, he enrolled in the University of Utah, although he never received a degree. Rather than staying in college, he decided to pursue a career in politics and political consultancy, which set him up for future success in the industry.

3. connections: Throughout his life, Rove has experienced both joy and difficulty in his connections, particularly those with his spouses and kids. Despite facing personal challenges, Rove has managed to find love and support in his relationships and has made an effort to retain close family ties despite the demands of his profession.

Karl Rove

All things considered, Karl Rove's family history has greatly influenced his political views, personal values, and professional path. His upbringing in a politically active family and managing interpersonal connections have shaped the way he approaches politics and public life.

7.2 Interests and Hobbies

In addition to his political career and strategic acumen, Karl Rove has a variety of interests and pastimes that shed light on his personal life away from politics. Karl Rove had the following interests and pastimes:

1. Reading: Rove is renowned for being a voracious reader with a broad interest in literature, politics, and history. He has been seen carrying books on a variety of subjects, and his political commentary and writing frequently refer to historical occasions and personalities.

2. Music: Rove loves to listen to music, especially country and classical styles. He has a broad interest in music that reaches many genres and eras, and he has been known to attend concerts and shows.

3. Playing the Guitar: Rove is a talented guitarist who has been spotted picking up the instrument on a few occasions. Rove enjoys listening to and playing music, and he has been known to do it both in private and in public.

4. Outdoor Activities: Cycling and hiking are two of Rove's favorite outdoor pursuits. He is well known for appreciating the natural beauty of the outdoors and has been sighted hiking in several places.

5. Dog Lover: Rove is a dog lover who has frequently been pictured with his furry friends. He has shown a fondness for dogs and is well-known for supporting causes related to animal welfare.

6. Travel: Rove has been to many places all over the world and enjoys traveling. He has taken many trips for business and pleasure, seeing new places and having exciting experiences.

7. Writing: Rove is a published author in addition to his political analysis and comments. He has authored multiple books on politics, history, and current affairs, utilizing his personal experiences and perceptions to provide readers with a more profound comprehension of the political terrain.

In general, Karl Rove's interests and pastimes are a reflection of his wide range of outside interests and passions. Even though Rove is most renowned for his work as a political analyst and strategist, he has a wide range of hobbies and pursuits outside of politics that help shape his character and personality.

CONCLUSION

We have explored the complex life and career of one of the most significant political strategists of our day in Karl Rove: Inside the Mind of a Political Genius. We have learned about Karl Rove's political acumen, controversies, and long-lasting influence on US politics through this investigation.

As our tour through Rove's head comes to an end, a few important revelations surface. First off, the electoral landscape has changed as a result of Rove's unmatched mastery of campaign strategy and messaging, which has helped the Republican Party win multiple local, state, and national elections. His ground-breaking application of voter outreach, microtargeting, and data analytics has revolutionized political campaigns and permanently altered the face of contemporary politics.

Still, there is some dispute over Rove's legacy. Questions have been raised concerning the ethics and integrity of

Karl Rove

his approach to politics due to his aggressive methods, nasty campaigning style, and involvement in political scandals. His reputation has been damaged by accusations of partisanship, manipulation, and unethical behavior, which have also spurred discussions about the nature of political discourse in the United States.

Rove continues to have a significant impact on American politics despite these scandals. Elections, policy discussions, and public opinion are all impacted by his media presence, policy advocacy, and strategic savvy, which continue to affect the political landscape. The lasting influence of individuals on the path of history and the potency of political strategy is demonstrated by Rove's legacy.

Ultimately, Karl Rove: Inside the Mind of a Political Genius presents a deep and multifaceted picture of a man whose influence goes beyond party politics. Rove's influence will endure in the corridors of power and in the minds of those who research the art and science of political strategy, whether they are applauded or not.

Karl Rove